Joomla!™ 3
in 10 easy steps

Author: Hagen Graf

cocoate

cover design:
Jade Black Design

Joomla! 3
in 10 Easy Steps

The new Joomla! 3.x series is mobile ready and comes with a complete new user interface. The book covers the standard term support release Joomla! 3.0

Learn in 10 easy steps to install, configure, and maintain your Joomla! website

1. What is Joomla?

Joomla is a free system for creating websites. It is an open source project, which, like most open source projects, is constantly in motion. It has been extremely successful for seven years now and is popular with millions of users worldwide.

The word Joomla is a derivative of the word Jumla from the African language Swahili and means "all together".

The project Joomla is the result of a heated discussion between the Mambo Foundation, which was founded in August 2005, and its then-development team. Joomla is a development of the successful system Mambo. Joomla is used all over the world for simple homepages and for complex corporate websites as well. It is easy to install, easy to manage and very reliable.

The Joomla team has organized and reorganized itself throughout the last seven years to better meet the user demands.

VERSION STRATEGY

Joomla versions are either standard term or long term supported (STS and LTS). A standard term supported release is good for 7 months, a long term release for 22 months. Every 6 months a new STS will be released

You can recognize a long term release by the .5 in the version.

• Joomla 2.5 is the actual long term support release and will be replaced by Joomla 3.5 in September 2013

• Joomla 3.0 is the actual standard term support release and will be replaced by Joomla 3.1 in March 2013

• Joomla 3.1 will be the next standard term supported release from March 2013 to September 2013

• Joomla 3.5 will be the next standard term supported release from September 2013 to March 2015

Long term releases are the proposed path for productive websites.

Standard term releases are a kind of playground for site builders and developers and if you start to build a website from scratch the proposed entry point (*Figure 1*).

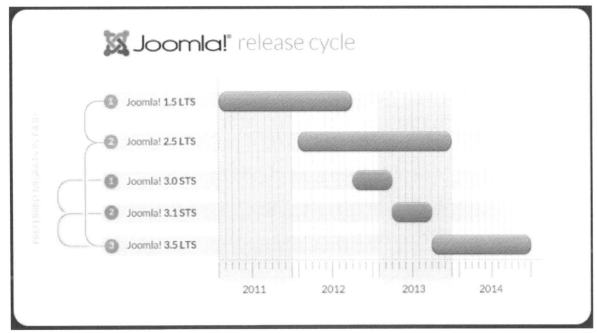

Figure 1: Joomla Release Cycle 2011-2014 (by Pawel Borowicz)

WHICH VERSION OF JOOMLA IS THIS BOOK ABOUT?

This book covers the standard term release Joomla 3.0 released in September 2012.

DO I HAVE TO UPGRADE MY OLD SITE?

Usually there are three different possibilities:

1. If your website is still in the LTS Joomla 1.5 branch, then it might be a good idea to upgrade it to the LTS Joomla 2.5 or start from scratch with the fresh STS Joomla 3 and follow the upgrades in the 3.x series up to LTS Joomla 3.5.

2. If your website is already made with LTS Joomla 2.5 then there is no need to upgrade now. There will be a defined upgrade path to the next LTS Joomla 3.5 in September 2013.

3. If you start to build a website now then it's a good idea to start with the STS Joomla 3.0.

WHAT'S NEW IN JOOMLA 3.0?

There are many improvements behind the scenes.
The most significant changes for site builders and users are:

• Joomla goes mobile with new responsive templates. Your Joomla website will be displayed nicely on every mobile device browser (Figure 2).
Joomla has a new user interface

• Joomla uses the JavaScript library jQuery

- The web installer is easier and only a 3 steps procedure

- Language packages can be installed directly from the extension manager (*Figure 3*)

- Smart Search, which was introduced with Joomla 2.5 got many improvements

- TinyMCE WYSIWYG Editor comes in a newer version (3.5.6)

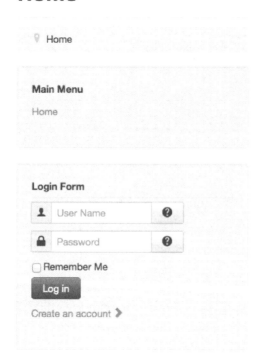

Figure 2: Joomla! on a mobile device

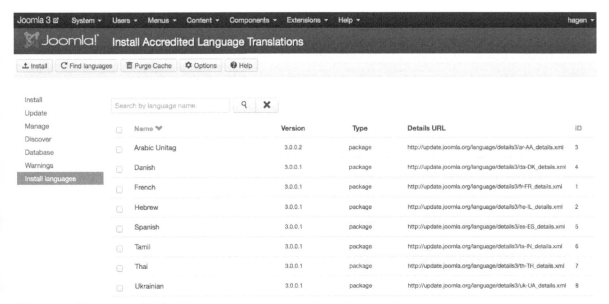

Figure 3: Language Packages

Some technical changes are not that visible but more than useful and appreciated

- Saving blank articles allowed

- Joomla is coming with a PostgreSQL Driver. You will be able to run Joomla 3.0 sites using the PostgreSQL database.

- With the PHP Memcached Driver Joomla performance can be accelerated

- Use of another library (JFeed) for feed management rather than SimplePie

- Continued clean up of older unused code, files and database fields and tables and improved standardization of tables.

- Extensive work on code style standardisation and consistency

- Unit testing in the CMS

- Updated system tests in the CMS

  and many more

WHAT CAN YOU DO WITH JOOMLA?

All kinds of dynamic websites can be created with Joomla. These websites consists of web pages containing content such as text, images, video and audio. The pages changes or customizes themselves frequently and automatically, based on certain criteria. Take the frontpage as an example. Usually it displays the newest articles automatically on top.

As all the sites in the world wide web are based on the same principles websites can be roughly divided in

Blogs (web logs)

A blog is a discussion or informational site consisting of articles (posts, blog entries). The most recent articles appears first.

Example: http://www.joomlablogger.net/

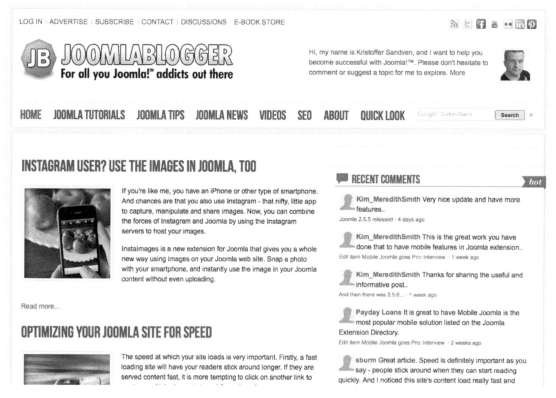

Figure 4: joomlablogger.net

Brand building sites

A site with the purpose of creating an experience of a brand online. These sites usually do not sell anything, but focus on building the brand.

Example: http://www.ihop.com/

Figure 5: ihop.com

Brochure websites

A brochure website include information about a company and its products and services through text, photos, animations, audio/video and interactive menus and navigation.

Example: http://www.solesolutions.no/

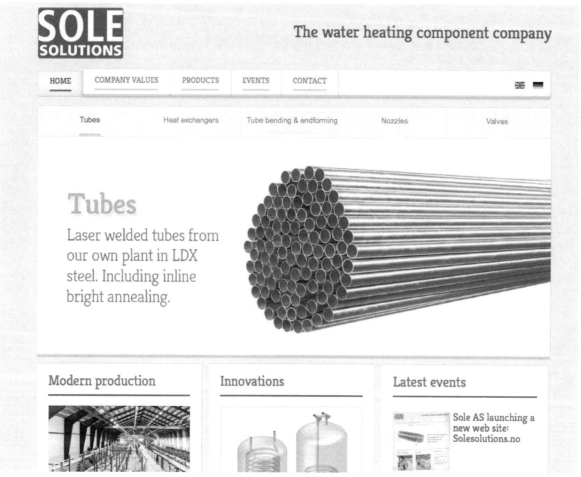

Figure 6: solesolutions.no

Celebrity sites

Disclaimer: the definiton of a celibrity can be complicate :)

A website whose information revolves around a celebrity. This sites can be official or fan made.

Example: http://www.deep-purple.com/

Figure 7: deep-purple.com

Community sites

A site where persons with similar interests communicate with each other.

Example: http://www.starvmax.com/community

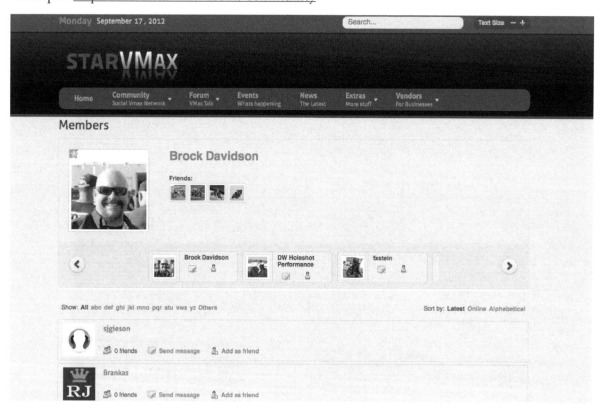

Figure 8: starvmax.com/community

Electronic commerce sites

A site offering goods and services for online sale and enabling online transactions for such sales. Example: http://regalosdecocina.com/

Figure 9: regalosdecocina.com

Forum websites

A site where people discuss various topics.

Example: http://www.sol.dk/debat/kategorier

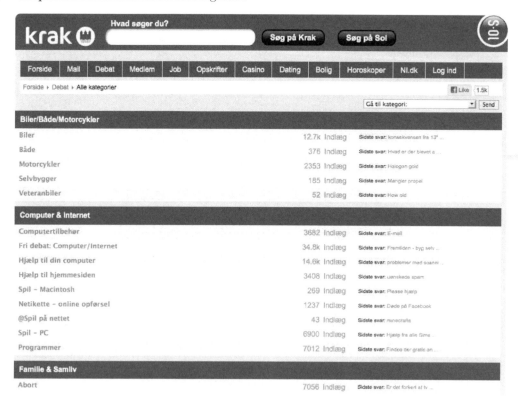

Figure 10: www.sol.dk/debat/kategorier

Gallery websites

A website designed specifically for use as a Gallery, these may be an art gallery or photo gallery and of commercial or non-commercial nature.

Example: http://www.mb-photography.com/

Figure 11: www.mb-photography.com

Government sites

More than 3,000 government websites around the world are built with Joomla.

Examples: http://joomlagov.info/

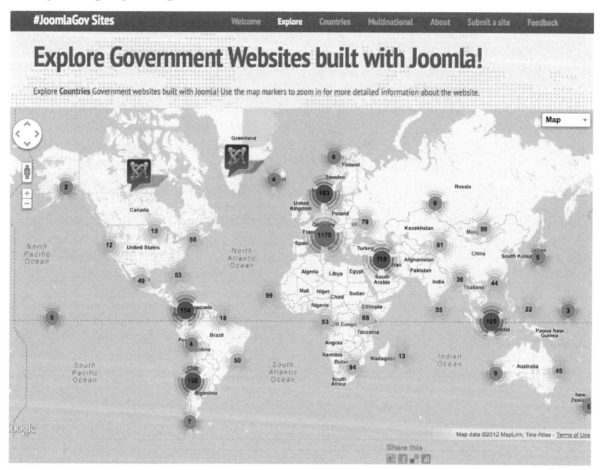

Figure 12: joomlagov.info

News sites

Similar to an information site, but dedicated to dispensing news, politics, and commentary.
Example: http://www.aa.com.tr/

Figure 13: www.aa.com.tr/

Personal websites

Websites about an individual or a small group (such as a family) that contains information or any content that the individual wishes to include.

Example: http://www.ilnono.it/it/

Figure 14: hwww.ilnono.it

600,000,000 WEBSITES

Did you ever ask yourself How Many Websites Are There in 2012? There are a lot, but nobody knows the exact answer to that question.

As you may have noticed, most of the example sites are not the big fishes in the world wide web but they fulfil the needs of their creators and their clients. This does not mean, that Joomla is only useful for smaller websites, it just means that most of the websites are made with limited resources on time and budget and for that reason people often build them with open source systems like Joomla, WordPress and Drupal.

Bigger websites like Facebook, Flickr, YouTube, Google, Apple, or Microsoft are usually not using one open source content management system for their websites. These companies usually have thousands of developers that create often hundred of websites by selecting and combining all the ideas and solutions available on the market. It is usually not about the technique, it's more about business models and ideas.

AMATEURS VERSUS PROFESSIONALS

The above listed websites are created by people that I want to divide in amateurs and professionals.

- Amateurs are trying to get around. They usually do not want to know one's stuff, they are happy if succeeded.

- Professionals try to get to the ground of what they are doing to be able to provide solutions which can be optimized over time. They try to transfer knowledge to strengthen others and build their business around the topic.

For Joomla it doesn't matter whether you are an amateur or a professional. Both can deal with Joomla and often amateurs become professionals over time and professionals start to get more involved to make Joomla CMS and Framework better and better.
Time for the first and the last advice in this book!

> *Ignore people talking about what you have to do. Focus on moving toward what you like to do instead*

WHAT ARE THE COMMON PARTS IN ALL THESE WEBSITES?

Even if the listed example websites are all very different, they have a few things in common:

- they are displaying content (text, images, video, audio)

- they have individual designs, layouts and colors. Individual doesn't mean perfect or tasteful or artistic. It just means "individual" :)

- visitors can interact in some ways with the site. Sometimes they have to create a user account in advance

- the common static words are available in different languages, sometimes the content too.

JOOMLA IS THE GLUE

All these websites are based on the ideas of their creators and the almost endless possibilities of the Joomla Content Management System. In this book, I want to cover the common parts of all these websites. You'll be able to create a quite nice looking website on your own after you have read the next 9 chapters. And it's up to you, whether you do it in the amateur or in the professional way :)

2. Download and Install Joomla

Panic …. where and what to download? Where to install? Why installing? What do I install?

In order to install Joomla! on your local PC, it is necessary to set up your "own internet", for which you'll need a browser, a web server, a PHP environment and as well a Joomla supported database system. We call this a solution stack and a client server system.

A solution stack is a set of software subsystems or components to make a fully functional Joomla website possible.

The solution stack we need consists of

- the operating system (Linux, Windows, OSX)

- the web server (Apache, IIS)

- the database (MySQL, PostgreSQL)

- the script language (PHP)

You can build a solution stack on your own machine at home or you can buy or rent it from a hosting company in different "flavours". The specific requirements for Joomla 3.x are described in *Table 1*.

Software	Minimum
PHP	5.3.1 +
MySQL (InnoDB support required)	5.1 +
Apache (with mod_mysql, mod_xml, and mod_zlib	2.x +)
Microsoft IIS	7

Table 1: Requirements for Joomla 3.x

Since this issue is the same for all PHP-based systems, I would like to refer you to the chapter installation variants of PHP-based systems [1].

If the solution stack is up and running, we call the result a server. The server can be your local computer or any other computer. All the visitors and users of the website are using a browser on their computer to access your Joomla site. We call them clients.

The "classic" LAMP stack looks like in Figure 1.

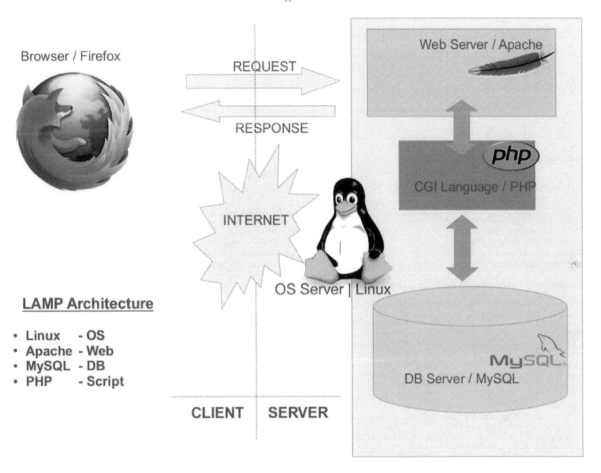

Figure 1: LAMP solution stack (graphic Wikipedia[2])

THE JOOMLA WEB INSTALLER

Thanks to the web installer, Joomla! can be installed in only a few minutes.
The Joomla! files will be copied to the public document root folder and configured with the Joomla! web

---

[1] http://cocoate.com/node/6540

[2] http://en.wikipedia.org/wiki/LAMP_%28software_bundle%29

installer.

Download Joomla! 3 from joomla.org[3] and unpack the files into your public document root folder of the web server (e.g.: */htdocs*).

From now on, everything is going really fast because the Joomla! web installer is working for you. Go to URL *http://localhost/*.

STUMBLING BLOCKS

This topic is very complex because there is a vast number of providers and an even greater number of installed web server, PHP, MySQL versions and web space management tools. Crunch points during the installation often consist of:

- an activated PHP Safe Mode, preventing you to upload files,

- 'forbidden' rewrite paths with the Apache web server because the so-called Apache Rewrite Engine (mod_rewrite) is not activated,

- the directory permissions on Linux and OSX, which are set differently than in Windows.

Basically, the easiest way that almost always works is the following:

- Download the current file package from Joomla.org to your home PC and unzip everything into a temporary directory.

- Load the unpacked files via FTP onto your rented server or to the directory of your local installation. The files must be installed in the public directory. These directories are usually called htdocs, public_html or html. If there are already other installations in that directory, you can specify a subdirectory in which your Joomla files should be installed. Many web hosts allow you to link your rented domain name to a directory.

- You have to find out the name of your database. In most cases, one or more databases are included in your web hosting package. Sometimes, the names of the user, database and password are already given; sometimes you have to set them up first. Usually you can do this in a browser-based configuration interface. You will need the database access information for Joomla!'s web installer.

PRE-INSTALLATION CHECK

The pre installation check helps you to verify whether your server environment is suitable for the installation of Joomla!. It appears with a selection of languages. As long as you see a red marker, your solution stack is not configured in a proper way and the installer refuses to install Joomla. Depending on your configuration, there can be differences. The Joomla! Installer considers the configuration settings of the web server (in our case Apache), PHP, and the operating system. When using Unix-like Systems

---

[3] http://www.joomla.org/download.html

(Linux, Mac OS X), you have to pay attention to file permissions[4]. This is particularly important for the file configuration.php. This file will be generated at the end of the installation with your personal values. If the installer can not write in the folder, Joomla! can not be created. In this case, configure the rights and then click the button repeat check.

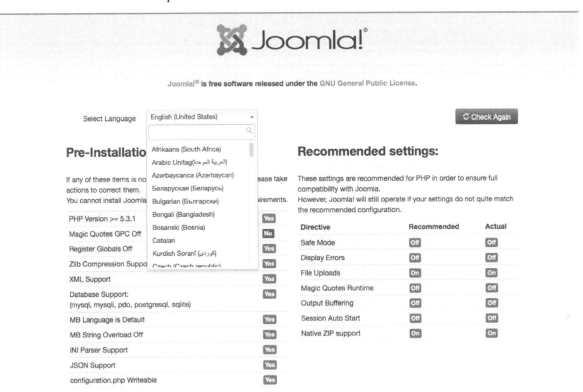

Figure 2: Pre Installation Check

STEP 1 – CONFIGURATION

In the main configuration window you have to describe your site and the administrator user. Furthermore, there is a switch to decide whether your site will be immediately visible for visitors (online) or if it will display a maintenance page (offline). This configuration setting is useful when you install Joomla directly in your live hosting environment (*Figure 3*).

---

[4] http://cocoate.com/node/3232

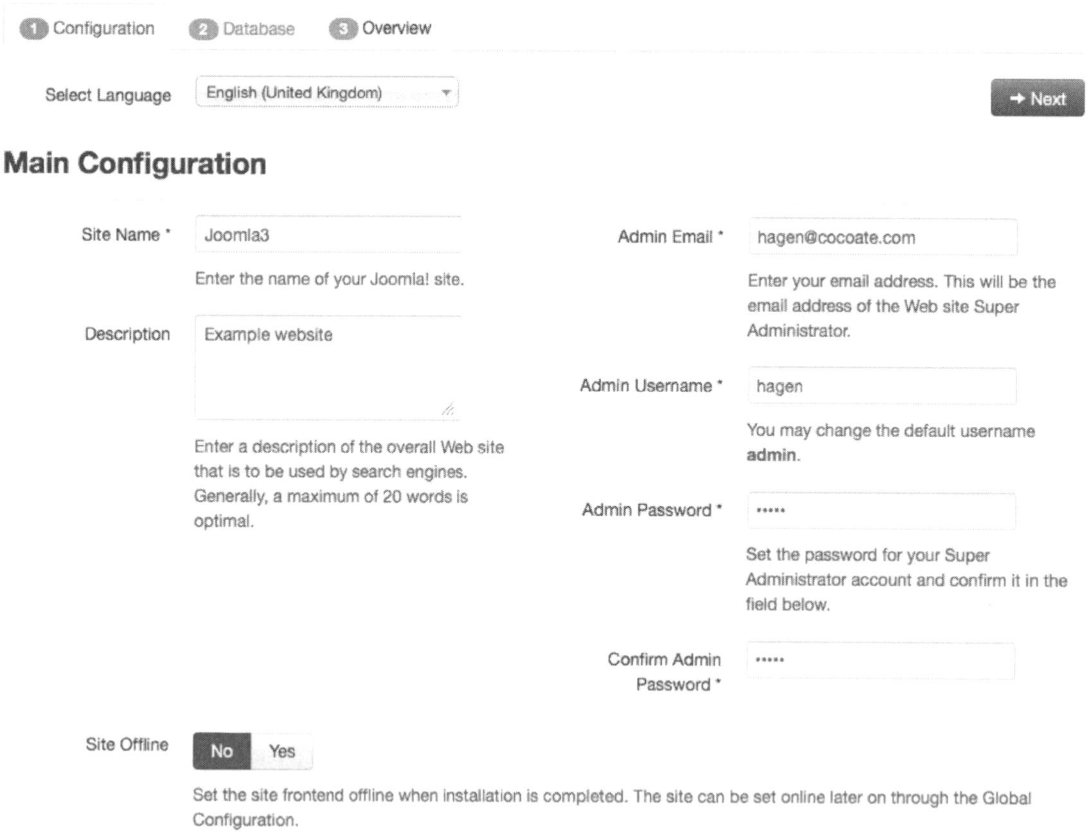

① Configuration   ② Database   ③ Overview

Select Language   English (United Kingdom) ▾   **→ Next**

Main Configuration

Site Name *   Joomla3

Enter the name of your Joomla! site.

Description   Example website

Enter a description of the overall Web site that is to be used by search engines. Generally, a maximum of 20 words is optimal.

Admin Email *   hagen@cocoate.com

Enter your email address. This will be the email address of the Web site Super Administrator.

Admin Username *   hagen

You may change the default username **admin**.

Admin Password *   •••••

Set the password for your Super Administrator account and confirm it in the field below.

Confirm Admin Password *   •••••

Site Offline   **No**   Yes

Set the site frontend offline when installation is completed. The site can be set online later on through the Global Configuration.

Figure 3: Installer - Main Configuration

STEP 2 – DATABASE

You can use various database servers with Joomla and you have to decide which database server you want to use and you need to enter your database parameters (Figure 4). In your local server environment you can create any number of databases.

In the MAMP package and in Ubuntu Linux, you have a MySQL user with the name root. The user root is the MySQL administrator and can, therefore, do everything in your MySQL system. The password depends on your server environment (no password is needed with XAMPP[5], with MAMP[6] the password is *root* too).

When you are in a live hosting environment these parameters will be given to you by your provider.

---

[5] http://www.apachefriends.org/

[6] http://www.mamp.info/

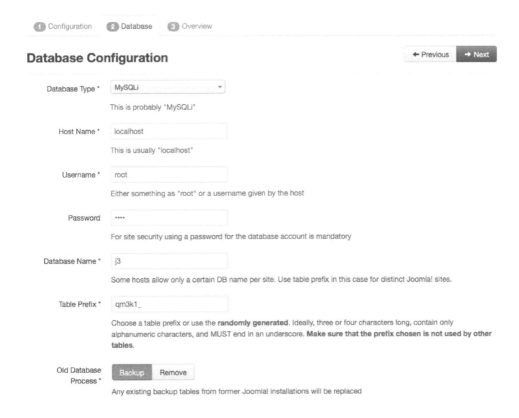

Figure 4: Installer – Database Configuration

Enter the following values into your local installation:

- computer name: localhost

- user name: root

- password: [only you know that]

Now select the database name. In a productive environment on a database server with a provider, you probably have a fixed quota of databases and the database credentials are predefined. If you have root permission on your database server, you can enter a name of a new database. Joomla! will then create that database. You can select whether the tables of any existing Joomla! installation in this database should be cleared or saved and marked with the prefix *bak_*. The table prefix is really practical. In front of each table name generated by the web installer, it writes the text that you typed in the appropriate field. As a default, the web installer suggests a randomly created one, like *w02rh_* . This has a simple reason. Sometimes you may only be able to get one MySQL database from your provider. If you want to run two or more Joomla! sites, you have a problem, as the tables do not differ from each other. With the table prefix it is possible to distinguish several tables (*w01client_* or *w02client_*). Here, you should use the default *w02rh_* . The prefix is also used to indicate saved data (*bak_*), see above.

STEP 3 – FINALISATION

In the third step, Joomla summarizes the configuration settings and asks if you want to install sample data (*Figure 4*).

① Configuration ② Database ③ Overview

Finalisation

← Previous → Install

Install Sample Data
- ⦿ None
- ○ Blog English (GB) Sample Data
- ○ Brochure English (GB) Sample Data
- ○ Default English (GB) Sample Data
- ○ Learn Joomla English (GB) Sample Data
- ○ Test English (GB) Sample Data

Installing sample data is strongly recommended for beginners.
This will install sample content that is included in the Joomla! installation package.

Overview

Email Configuration **No** Yes

Select to email below configuration settings to `hagen@cocoate.com` after installation.

Main Configuration

Site Name	Joomla3
Description	Example website
Site Offline	No
Admin Email	hagen@cocoate.com
Admin Username	hagen
Admin Password	***

Database Configuration

Database Type	mysqli
Host Name	localhost
Username	root
Password	***
Database Name	j3
Table Prefix	qm3k1_
Old Database Process	Backup

Pre-Installation Check

PHP Version >= 5.3.1	Yes
Magic Quotes GPC Off	Yes
Register Globals Off	Yes
Zlib Compression Support	Yes
XML Support	Yes
Database Support: (mysql, mysqli, pdo, postgresql, sqlite)	Yes
MB Language is Default	Yes
MB String Overload Off	Yes
INI Parser Support	Yes
JSON Support	Yes
configuration.php Writeable	Yes

Recommended settings:

These settings are recommended for PHP in order to ensure full compatibility with Joomla.
However, Joomla! will still operate if your settings do not quite match the recommended configuration.

Directive	Recommended	Actual
Safe Mode	Off	Off
Display Errors	Off	Off
File Uploads	On	On
Magic Quotes Runtime	Off	Off
Output Buffering	Off	Off
Session Auto Start	Off	Off
Native ZIP support	On	On

Figure 4: Finalisation

In former versions of Joomla it was only possible to install ONE set of sample data. With Joomla 3 it is possible to choose of several sample data sets. The "sample data system" can be used to configure a predefined site layout and example content for a weblog (*Figure 5*), a brochure site (*Figure 6*), a "*Learn Joomla*" site with a Joomla tutorial inside (*Figure 7*) and the default site (*Figure 8*).

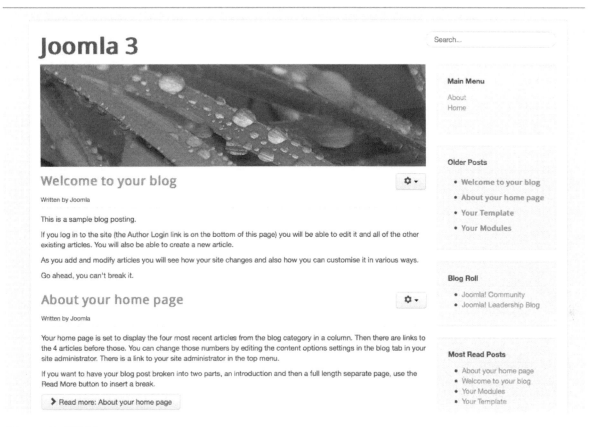

Figure 5: Weblog

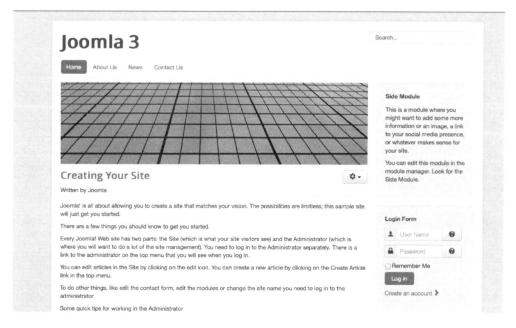

Figure 6: Brochure Website

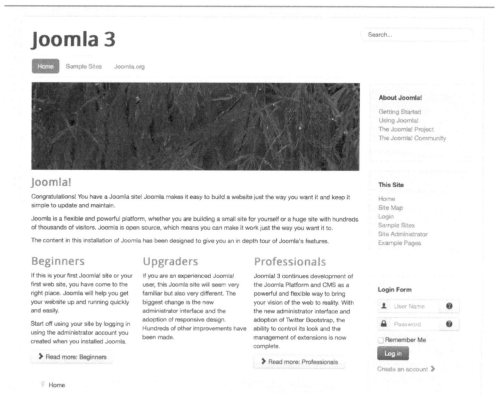

Figure 7: Learn Joomla

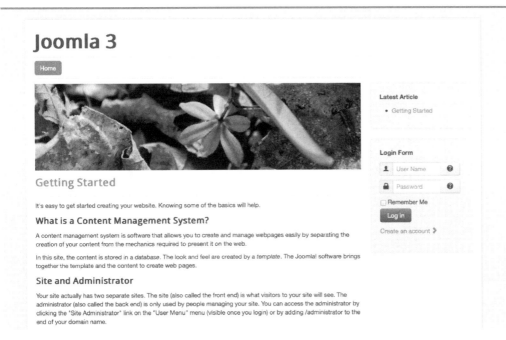

Figure 8: Default

Depending on your needs and your knowledge, you should try the different sample data sets. Unfortunately it's not possible to switch between the different sample data sets after the installation is finished.

It's also possible to install Joomla without any sample data. The "empty Joomla" is a good start for your website if you already know how to use Joomla.

I'm choosing a naked Joomla without any sample data as a base for the next chapters.

You'll be able to understand and follow the chapters without of the pre-installed sample data.

So choose the sample data you want to use and click the Install button. Joomla creates the database and configures the site for you (*Figure 9*).

Figure 9: Joomla! is now installed

For security reasons, it's necessary to remove the installation folder by clicking the *Remove installation folder* button. After the removal of the installation folder it is possible to view the site and to enter the administration area (*/administrator*). In my case the site looks like in *Figure 10*.

Joomla 3

Home

♀ Home

Main Menu
Home

Login Form

👤 User Name ❷

🔒 Password ❷

☐ Remember Me

Log in

Create an account ❯

© Joomla 3 2012   Back to top

Figure 10: Joomla Website without sample data

The Joomla control panel can be accessed by pointing to

```
http://your_domain.tld/administrator
```

A login screen appears with the possibility to choose a preferred language (*Figure 11*) and after a successful login you'll see the administration area (*Figure 12*).

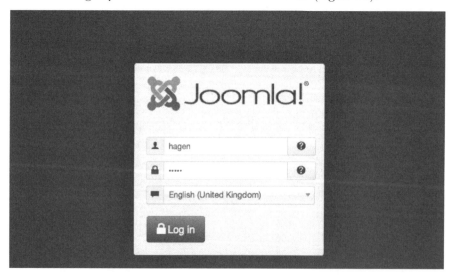

Figure 11: Login Screen

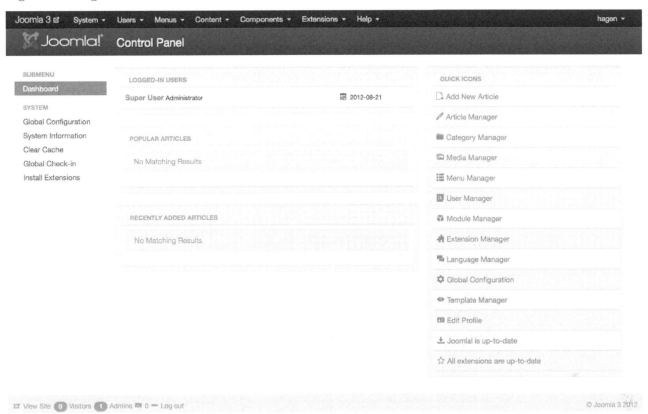

Figure 12: Control Panel

3. Joomla in your language

So far, your site and the control panel are available in British English only. This is Joomla's basic language. The language selection in the installer is just for the installation process.

As many of the Joomla installations are in countries that speak other languages than English, this topic is very important.

THE LANGUAGE MANAGER

In this first step we want to configure Joomla in your preferred language. That means, our Joomla site won't be available in several languages, just in the one chosen language.

The Language Manager (*Extensions → Language Manager*) the topic is divided into four displays:

1. Installed - Site

A list of installed languages on the website. You can set one language as default and activate and deactivate other languages (*Figure 1*)

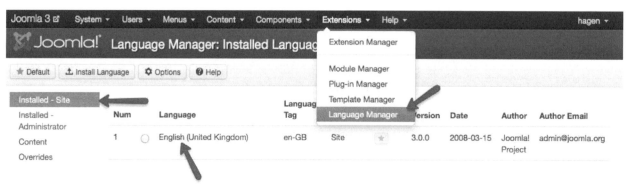

Figure 1: Site language

2. Installed - Administrator

A list of installed languages on the control panel. You can set one language as default and activate and deactivate other languages (*Figure 2*)

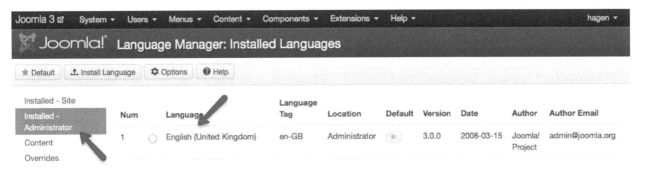

Figure 2: Control Panel Language

3. Content

Here you can set e.g. a site name, metadata options, the language code for each language version (*Figure 3*).

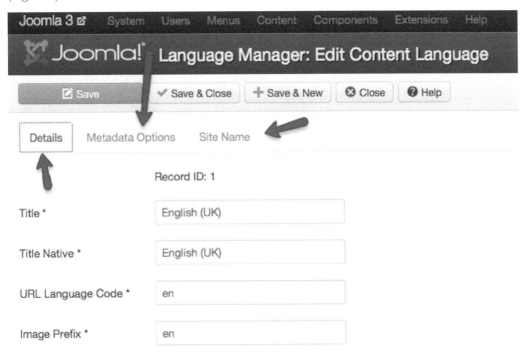

Figure 3: Language parameters for a single language

4. Overrides

You can override the standard language strings. This is a very useful feature if you need to change only a few words.

The Joomla language system stores sentences like "Please login to view the article" in variables like

COM_CONTENT_ERROR_LOGIN_TO_VIEW_ARTICLE. If you are not happy with that sentence you can override it (Figure 4). It is possible to search for text strings.

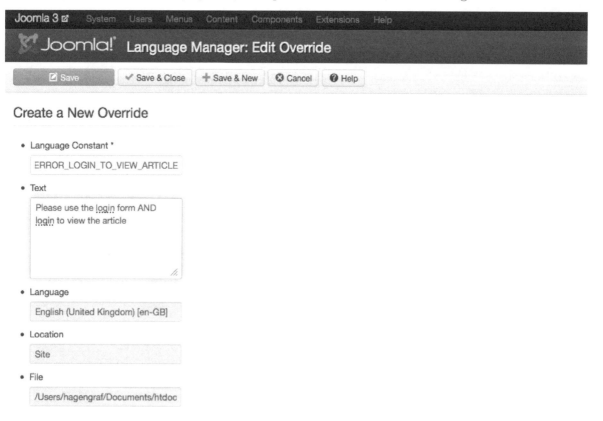

Figure 4: Language Overrides

INSTALL A NEW LANGUAGE

Click the Install Language button in the language manager and Joomla sends you to *Extensions →
Extension Manager → Install Languages*. If you are there for the first time you should see all the available language packages. Choose your desired language and click the install button. (*Figure 5*).

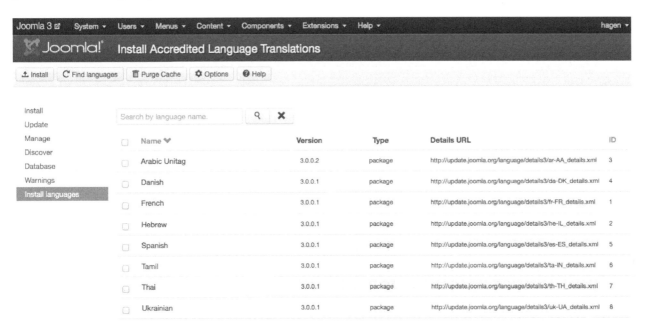

Figure 5: Available Language Packages

Go back to the language manager (*Extensions → Language Manager*) and set your language as the default language for the site and the control panel, deactivate English and you are done

Figure 6: The control panel in Spanish

A detailed description of a multilingual environment is covered in this chapter[7] and this screencast[8]. Both are based on Joomla 1.7/2.5 but the general behavior in Joomla 3 is exactly the same.

---

[7] http://cocoate.com/node/10332

[8] http://cocoate.com/node/10104

4. Design, Layout, Colors

The template is one of the most important pieces of a website. It provides the appearance, the design. It motivates new visitors to stay on your site and explore. Regular visitors and users appreciate being on a site with a beautiful and useful design. Think of other products, for instance. A car needs a good engine and tires but one of the most important reasons for buying one is often the design. Even if the design is not the main reason, it is often a trigger to contemplate the idea of purchasing and may cause a buyer to consider more tangible reasons. If the design is well-made, people expect the rest to be well-made, too. (*Figure 1, Figure 2*)!

Figure 1: Car with stickers (photo Richardmasoner[9])

Figure 2: Red car (FotoSleuth)[10]

---

[9] http://www.flickr.com/photos/bike/201402884

[10] http://www.flickr.com/photos/51811543@N08/4978639642

Both of these cars are made for different target groups. They are an example of different approaches in design.

A FEW DEFINITIONS

I just want to clarify a few terms to sensitize your thinking

What is design?

• The noun design stands for a plan or drawing which shows the function and the lookout of an object, to accomplish particular goals in a particular environment and to satisfy a set of requirements

• the verb "to design"stands for creating a design, in an environment (where the designer operates)

The term design can be used in

• art ("almost instinctive", "built-in", "natural", and part of "our sense of 'rightness'),

• engineering (product design of a new car)

• production (planning and executing)

• processes (business process modeling)

What is page layout?

Page layout is the part of "graphic" design that deals in the arrangement and style treatment of elements (content) on a page. To speak in Joomla terms, it is the arrangement of Joomla modules and the components on predefined templates positions.

What are colors?

Color is the visual perceptual property corresponding in humans to the categories called red, green, blue, and others. Individual colors have a variety of cultural associations such as national colors. There is great diversity in the use of colors and their associations between cultures and even within the same culture in different time periods.

HTML colors[11] and CSS colors[12] can have 16 million different values. The combination of Red, Green, and Blue values from 0 to 255, gives more than 16 million different colors (256 x 256 x 256).

Example: **BLACK** = color HEX #000000 = color RGB rgb(0,0,0)

Several tools like the color scheme designer[13] can help you to find the right colors for your website project (*Figure 3*).

---

[11] http://www.w3schools.com/html/html_colors.asp

[12] http://www.w3schools.com/cssref/css_colors.asp

[13] http://colorschemedesigner.com/

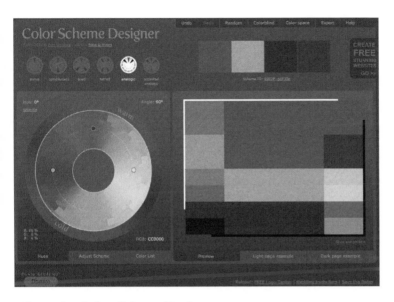

Figure 3: Color Scheme Designer

TEMPLATES

A template involves repeated elements visible to the visitors. Using a template to lay out elements usually involves less graphic design skill than that which was required to design the template. Templates are used for minimal modification of background elements and frequent modification (or swapping) of foreground content.

WEB DESIGN

Web design is somewhat like a handcraft and a broad term covering many different skills and disciplines that are used in the production and maintenance of websites.

Possessing skills in techniques like HTML, CSS, JavaScript, PHP, image editing and many others is imperative.

Joomla! is only one more tool in the web designers toolbox.

A good Joomla template is not only about colors and graphics. The shape and positioning of the content is just as important. The website has to be user-friendly and reliable. Exactly this challenge reminds me of the two cars again.

Web design is still a young profession. A web designer often has to deal with low bandwidth, incompatible browsers, inexperienced content editors and other people involved in the process of creating a 'good' website. The creation of a Joomla! website is often a process, in which everyone involved learns a lot. With Joomla 3, the project introduces the Joomla User Interface library (JUI) with the Protostar template.

Good web design is hard work! :-)

After having your site up in the language you prefer, most people start tweaking the colors and want to upload e.g. a new logo, even if there is no content so far. Joomla comes with preinstalled templates and so called template styles. A template style is a set of options (color, logo, layout) for a template. The configuration possibilities are depending on the template. Some template have a huge variety of settings and some are quite limited.

It is possible to create as many styles as you want and assign them to different pages of your website.

STRUCTURE

Joomla is known for its quality and simplicity. In Joomla a single page is generated by the HTML output of one component, several modules and the template. Each page is accessible via a unique URL. Take the front page as an example. The content component produces the HTML output for the articles in the middle. This screenshot is based on the Joomla Beez Template (Figure 4). The blocks next to the articles are different modules. You can combine the HTML output from one component with the HTML output of any number of modules. Existing modules can also be reused on other pages.

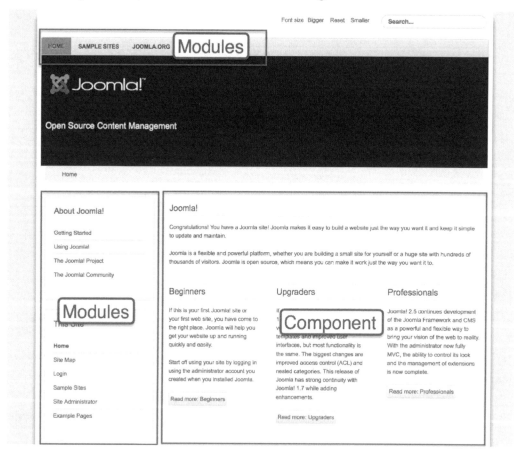

Figure 4: Joomla! front page

POSITIONS

You must know, of course, at which point you can assign modules at all. For this purpose, each template provides so-called positions. In order to see these positions you have to enable the Preview Module Positions switch (*Extensions* → *Template Manager* → *Options*). After that, you can access your website by using the parameter *tp=1* (*http://localhost/index.php?tp=1*) or click the Preview link in *Extensions* → *Templates Manager* → *Manager* (*Figure 5*).

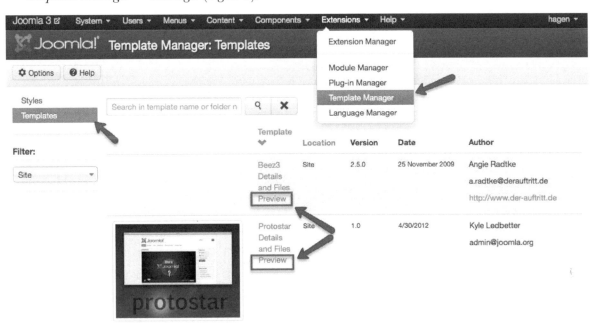

Figure 5: Template Manager - Site Templates

You'll see the emphasized module positions with their names (*Figure 6*).

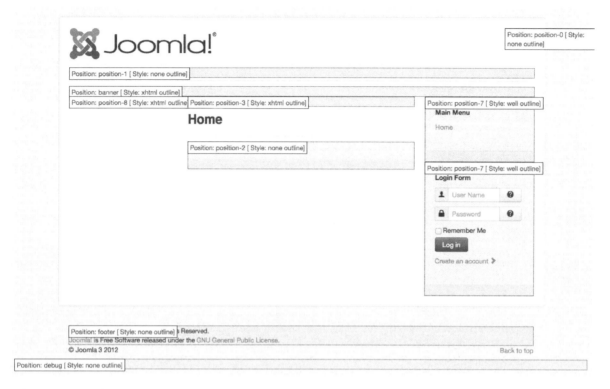

Figure 6: Module positions - Protostar template

In *Extensions* → *Module Manager* you can assign one of these positions to each module. If you need the module at different positions, you may also copy it.

CORE TEMPLATES

Joomla! core comes with two site templates and two administrator templates. You can see a preview in *Extensions* → *Template Manager* → *Tab Templates*. You can filter between Site and Administrator Styles by choosing the location filter (*Figure 6* and *Figure 7*).

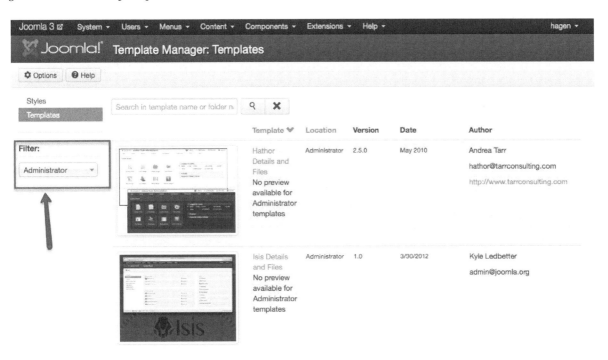

Figure 7: Template Manager - Administrator Templates

STYLES

Styles offers the possibility to create and use different versions of one template. A template has a minimum of one style. In this style, configurations can be made depending on the template, such as changing the colors or uploading the header logo. You may set the default style for your site in *Extensions → Template Manager → Styles*.

EXAMPLE: AN INDIVIDUAL STYLE

Let's create an individual style for our website:

• Name: cocoate

• Template Colour: #f88638

• Fluid Layout

You can create additional styles by copying them. For this example I filter for the Protostar template (*Figure 8*).

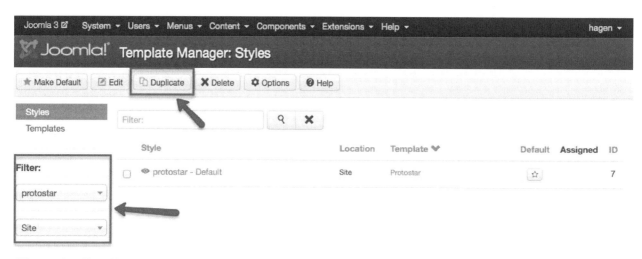

Figure 8 - Duplicate a style

Enter the name for the style and set it default for all languages. If you have a multilingual Joomla sites you can set different styles for different languages (*Figure 9*)

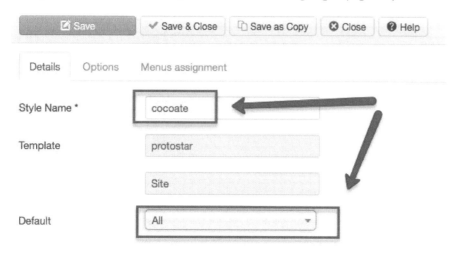

Figure 9 - Configuring a template style

In the Options tab you can choose a template and a background color, upload a logo and set the template either fix or fluid (*Figure 10*, *Figure 11*)

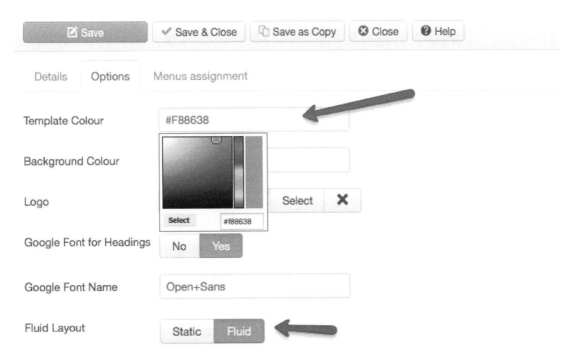

Figure 10 - Options tab - Style

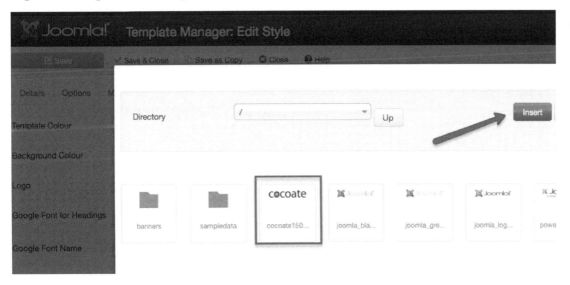

Figure 11 - Uploading a logo

Each style can be (has to be) assigned to a menu item. If you would like a green background on your site when people click on menu item A, for example, and a blue background when they click on menu item B, you can assign the corresponding styles. In my case I have only one menu item, because so far, we have no content on the site. I assign the new style to the Home menu item (*Figure 12*).

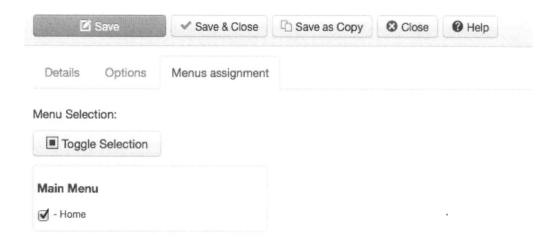

Figure 12 - Menu Assigments

After saving the style, the website looks different (*Figure 13*) and because the Protostar template is fully responsive, the website is shown perfectly on a mobile device too (*Figure 14*)

Figure 13 - The website on a desktop PC

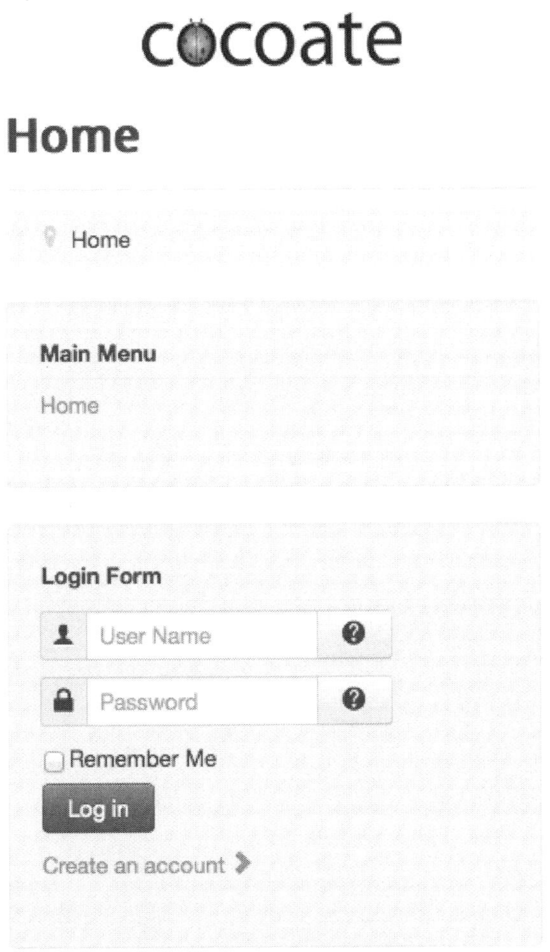

cocoate

Home

Home

Main Menu

Home

Login Form

👤 User Name ❓

🔒 Password ❓

☐ Remember Me

Log in

Create an account ❯

Figure 14 - The website on a mobile device

EDIT THE TEMPLATE FILES ONLINE

If you know the meaning of the abbreviations mentioned in the headline you can configure the templates directly. A template in Joomla is the base of a style and consists of various files. It's possible to change the central elements of a template online.

If you want to edit the Protostar template you have to access *Extensions* → *Template Manager* → *Templates* → *Protostar Details and Files* and click the link to the file.

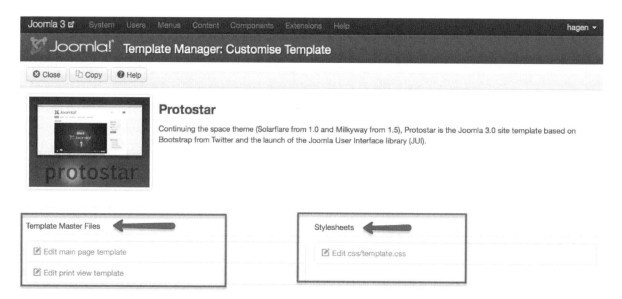

Figure 15: Edit Template files online

It's of course possible to edit the files in an external editor.

The site templates are located in the folder */templates*. Each template has it's own folder. Under the */templates/systems* folder you'll find the template files to edit the Offline and the Error page template. The admin templates are located in the folder */administrator/templates*.

5. It's all about users, permissions, modules and articles

I know, we still have no content on our site but before we create it, let's have a look on the user accounts of our new Joomla website.

When you installed Joomla, you created the Super Administrator account. This user can do anything. It is nice to be that user but it is dangerous too. You will probably have more than one user account on your website, e.g. authors who write articles. Let's build a platform for authors where they can post articles, upload images without the need to enter the Joomla's control panel. Follow the example and you'll learn a lot about Joomla :)

ABOUT USERS, ROLES AND PERMISSIONS

Before we start, it is important to know that

• users are in general able to login on the frontend and/or the control panel just depending on their role permissions.

• a user account has to be a member of a user group. Instead of assigning these permissions to each user, they are assigned to a group. The individual user is then assigned to one or more groups. Imagine you have 10,000 users in four different groups. It's easy for the administrator to change the permissions for each of the groups. Without groups, you would have to change every user account manually. However, when using groups, you only have to change permissions once!

Joomla comes with predefined groups like author and publisher which are easy to understand. An author is able to create/write something, a publisher has the additional permission to publish content.

• The predefined **frontend** user groups are: visitors, registered users, authors, editors, publishers

• The predefined **control panel** user groups are: manager, administrator, super administrator

EXAMPLE: A WEBSITE WHERE AUTHORS CAN POST ARTICLES

This is a very simple workflow but it covers a lot of possibilities that exist in Joomla. I assume that you have a "naked" Joomla without sample data and the super administrator user account.

The desirable scenario

- Admin user in control panel:
  - activates the admin notification when someone creates a new user account
  - creates a user menu for registered users with a link to create an article

- Visitor on website:

  registers as a new user

- Admin user in control panel:

  receives a notification and assigns the user to the authors group

- Author user on website:

  is able to create an article but is not allowed to publish it

- Admin user in control panel:
  - receives a notification that there is new content available
  - publishes the article on the frontpage

1. Administrator notification email and user menu

Go to *Users* → *User Manager* → *Options* and activate the Notification Mail to Administrators (*Figure 1*).

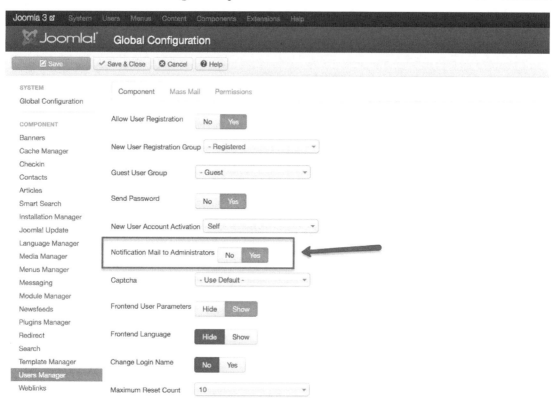

Figure 1: Notification Mail to Administrators

Go to *Menus* → *Menu Manager* and create a new menu:

- Title: User

- Menu Type: user

- Description: A menu for a user with useful links

Save and close it. You have created a kind of menu container. What's missing is the links inside the container and a linked module that displays the new menu at a certain position in the template. To create and link the module, click on the link Add a module for this menu type (*Figure 2*)

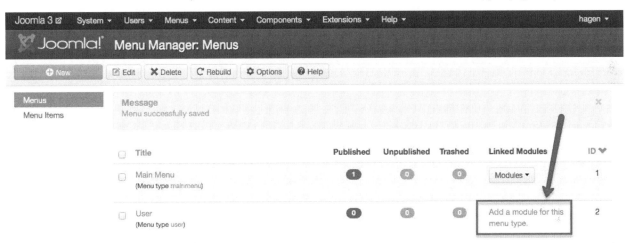

Figure 2: Add a module

In the module form you have to add a title (User Menu), the position (Right in the Protostar template), the access permission (registered users). Don't forget to save & close it (Figure 3).

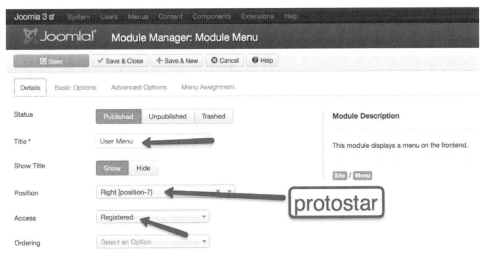

Figure 3: Creating the user menu module

Now we need the *"Create article"* link in our menu that should be shown to authors. Go to *Menus* → *User* → *new* (*Figure 4*)

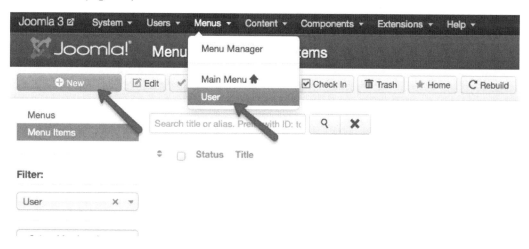

Figure 4: Creating a link in the user menu

In the following form you have to enter the name/description of the link (Menu Item Title), select a Menu Item Type (*Figure 5*) and restrict the access to registered users. Each Joomla component can provide Menu Item Types. Our type (create article) is provided by the content component which is a part of Joomla core.

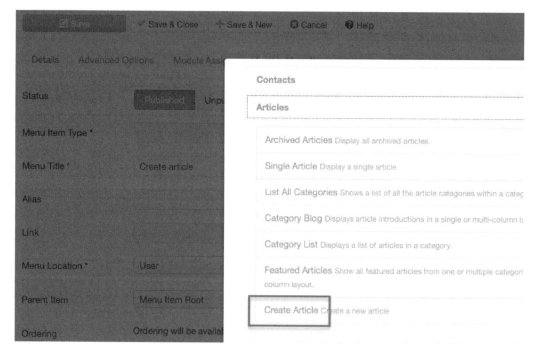

Figure 5: Select Menu Item Type

After you saved and closed the dialog a new menu item should be displayed in the list (*Figure 6*)

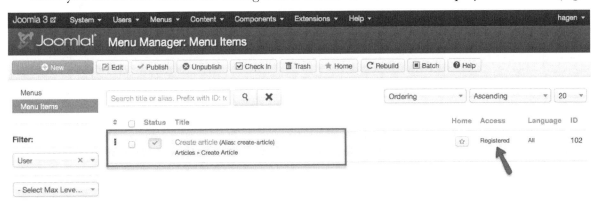

Figure 6: User Menu with the new menu item

Test your work! Login on the frontend with your Super Administrator account. After the login, our new user menu with the create link appears (*Figure 7*).

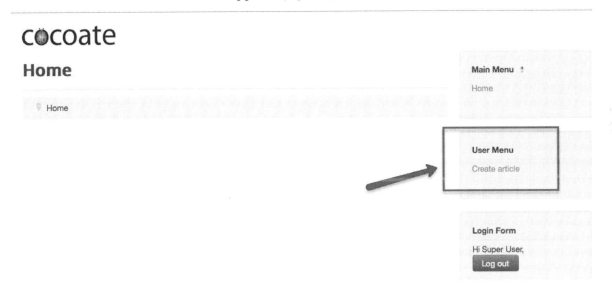

Figure 7: User Menu after Login

Please log out after the test.

2. Registration as a new user

Now we create a new user account. Please access the website as any other visitor and click the Create an account link. Fill out the form and click the Register button (*Figure 8*).

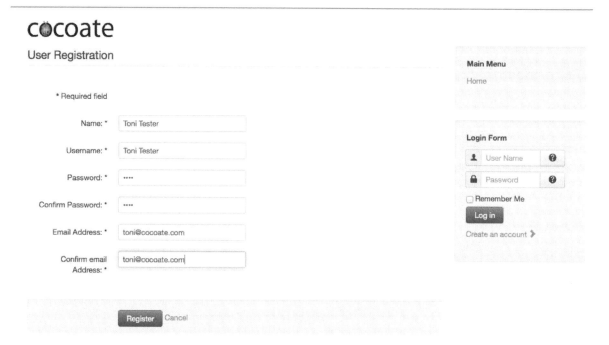

Figure 8: Registration form

If your server stack allows sending emails, a notification email will be send to the email address of the super administrator account.

Joomla offers a CAPTCHA to prevent spammers. To use it, activate the CAPTCHA plugin under *Extensions* → *Plugins* and select it in the options of the User Manager where you can configure the general behaviour of the login process too.

3. Assignment of the user to the authors group

Log in with your Administrator account on the control panel, access *Users* → *User Manager* and click on the name of the new user (*Toni Tester*). Check the Author group in the *Assigned User Groups* tab (*Figure 9*).

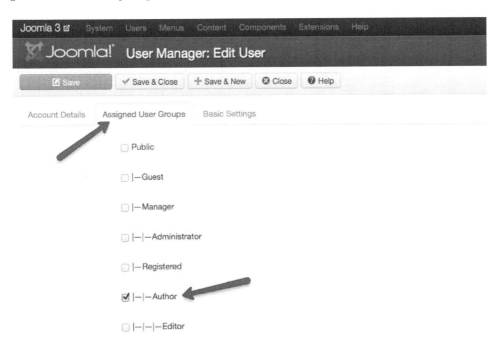

Figure 9: Assignment of a group to a user

4. Our new author creates an article

Log in with your new user account on the website and click the create article by just adding a title and a few words and click save (*Figure 10*).

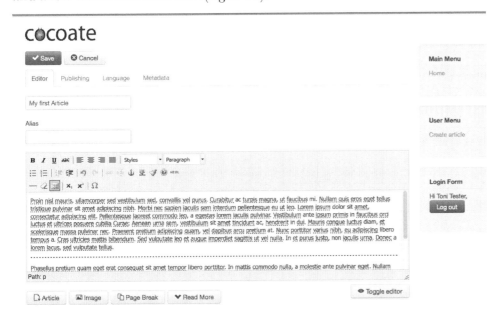

Figure 10: Create an article

The article is saved and submitted but the user (you) cannot see it, because it is not published. I configured this workflow intentionally as in some cases it is desired to have another person to edit the created content and then publish it.

Of course, it is also possible to skip that and the user to the group Publisher and then the article would be published immediately.

5. *The admin publishes the article on the frontpage*

Joomla comes with a messaging system and this system creates a message when new content was created by a user. Depending on your settings (*Components → Messaging → Options*) the admin receives that message by email or via the screen.

The admin has to go to *Content → Article Manager* and publish it. If the article should appear on the frontpage, click on featured. (*Figure 11, Figure 12*).

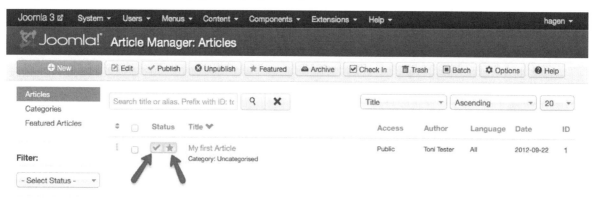

Figure 11: Publish an Article

Figure 12: Featured Article

Tweaking the process

As we already noticed while following this example, many topics are covered and the configuration is easily done depending on your needs. There is a huge amount of permissions, options and settings to discover. I'll provide a few examples in Chapter 8.

6. Create Content

Creating content is hard! Every piece of content is a story. And a story can be good or not that good and thus attracting visitors or bore them. Thousands of books on the subject of writing stories have been published, a lot of people have taught the lore.

I have a relatively easy task to cover just the technical part :)

WHAT IS AN ARTICLE IN JOOMLA?

Technically, an article consists of

- a title (headline) and an alias (in the url)

- the text (a mixture of text, images, and other media)

- a category where the article belongs to

- an author and an alias for the author

- access permissions

- a language the article is written in

- meta data for search engines and other robots

and a lot of options how, where, to whom and when the article is displayed.

You already wrote an article in the last chapter and this was not complicated. Just a title is necessary, all the other fields have a default value or are optional.

Let's go through this list :)

A Title

It's a little, but an important part.

It needs to be crisp and short to attracts readers and it's handy for you because the title appear in lists of articles on the website and as lists of articles in the control panel.

the title appears as the page title on top of your browser window and it can contain the site name too. You can configure this behaviour in

System → Global Settings → Site → SEO settings → Include Site Name in Page Titles

it can appear in the URL of that page (I) and it's up to you how to setup the URL

System → Global Settings → Site → SEO settings

The Text

In Joomla, the text of your article contains a part that is displayed in lists (teaser) and the rest of the article. This rest can be structured by page breaks, so that a long text results in 10 pages each with a table of content. But step by step :)

When you create an article you will do this with the help of an editor. Joomla uses a rich text editor (TinyMCE[14]). That means, it is not necessary for you as the author to learn HTML tags. The editor looks like a text processor window on your PC (e.g. Word, LibreOffice) and it is easy to understand the icons (*Figure 1*).

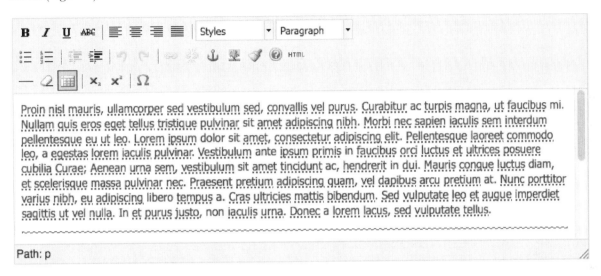

Figure 1: Rich text editor

If you hover over an icon with your mouse, there appears a tooltip with the description of the function the editor performs when the icon is clicked on

> *Note:*
>
> *It is possible to install different editors, for example the Joomla Content Editor[15] and it is also possible not to use any editor. Joomla itself comes with two editors and you can configure the default editor in System → Global Configuration → Site → Default Editor.*

The default settings allow your users to choose between the available editors by themselves in their user account. You can disable this feature in *Users → Users Manager → Options → Frontend User Parameters*.

Paste from Word

The worst case of editing happens, when people paste from programs like Microsoft Word. Even if the situation gets better there is still **NO REAL WAY** to get the same formats on a website that is based

---

[14] http://www.tinymce.com/

[15] http://www.joomlacontenteditor.net/

on HTML by pasting from a text processor like Microsoft Word that is based on binary formats or complicated XML. The editor offers a "Clean up messy code" icon but it will not clean up logical errors or differences in the markup. Keep that in mind when you talk to your users :)

Insert Images

At the bottom of the editor window you'll find a button called images. It offers a dialog to choose existing images from your inbuilt Joomla image library and it allows you to add images to this library by uploading them.

- You can manage your library under *Content → Media Manager*

- You can upload more than one file by enabling the flash uploader (*Content → Media Manager → Options → Enable Flash Uploader*)

- Joomla will not resize your images, so be careful with big photos! The best solution: your images have exactly the size in pixel you want to have them on your site. There are several extensions available for solving the resize issue and the Twitter Bootstrap framework that is used in Joomla 3, is helpful for responsive images.

After you have inserted an image from the library, you can configure (add attributes to) that image by clicking the image icon on top of the rich text editor (*Figure 2*)

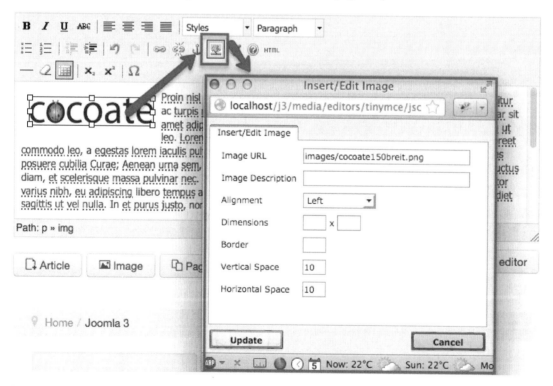

Figure 2: Using the rich text editor

References to other articles

The button *Article* at the bottom of the editor window allows to link from an article to another article which is quite useful.

Read more

Articles will appear in lists and on an article details page. On lists, the text should be limited to avoid confusion. With the help of the Read More button below the editor you limit the article text. Set the cursor in your text where the Read More break should appear and click the Read More button (*Figure 3*)

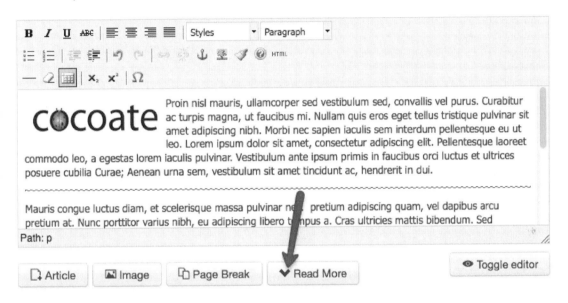

Figure 3: Read more link

EMBED A YOUTUBE VIDEO

This is not only about YouTube videos but it is a good example for text filters. If you try to embed a YouTube video with the typical code

```
<iframe width="560"
height="315"
src="http://www.youtube.com/embed/rX372ZwXOEM"
frameborder="0" allowfullscreen></iframe>
```

you notice that it is filtered by the editor and by Joomla. This is not a bug! It's a feature :)

For security reasons

Joomla uses so-called text filters (*System → Global Configuration → Text Filters*) to filter the following tags: *<applet>*, *<body>*, *<bgsound>*, *<base>*, *<basefont>*, *<embed>*, *<frame>*, *<frameset>*, *<head>*, *<html>*, *<id>*, *<iframe>*, *<ilayer>*, *<layer>*, *<link>*, *<meta>*, *<name>*, *<object>*, *<script>*, *<style>*, *<title>*, and *<xml>*.

TinyMCE filters some tags too: *<applet>*, *<object>* and *<iframe>*

Unfortunately, we need to insert an *<iframe>* tag to embed videos from YouTube.

So, how can the problem be solved?

One solution could be to trust your authors and create a custom blacklist (*System → Global Configuration → Text Filters*) for the authors group (*Figure 4*) and then tell TinyMCE the *<iframe>* is not evil anymore (*Extensions → Plug-in Manager → Editor-TinyMCE → Edit → Basic Options → Prohibited Elements*) by deleting the word iframe in the prohibited elements.

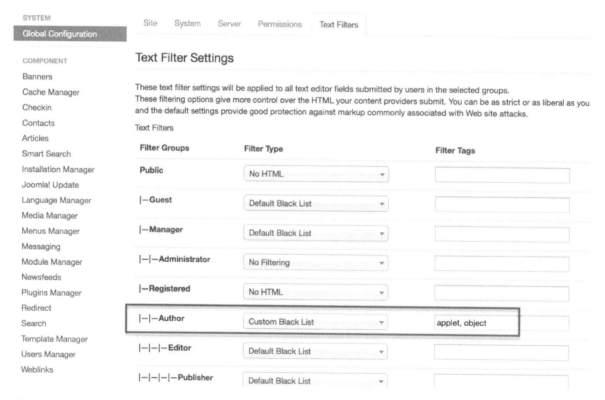

Figure 4: Custom Black List for the author group

After you have changed these filter mechanisms, it is possible to copy and paste the embed code into your article. Keep in mind that you need to switch the editor to the HTML view by clicking the HTML icon. Afterwards, a popup window with the HTML code of the article appears. Now paste the embed code where the video should appear (*Figure 5*).

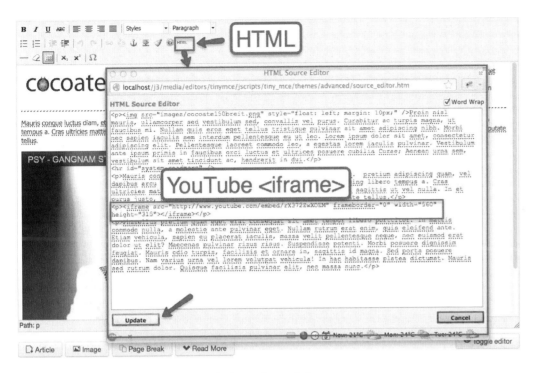

Figure 5: Inserting the iframe code into the article

Click the update button and you already can see the video inside the editor window. After saving the article the video will appear on your website (*Figure 6*).

Figure 6: Inserting the iframe code into the article

Now you can embed code from several platforms like Twitter, Facebook and Flickr.

Using macros in a text

It is possible to use so called macros in your text. A macro is an expression or command that is replaced with something different (e.g the embed code of your YouTube video).

Theoretically, we could write in our article text (not in the HTML) something like this

[youtube = http://www.youtube.com/watch?v=rX372ZwXOEM]

and some magic could replace this with the appropriate embed code

```
<iframe width="560" height="315" src="http://www.youtube.com/embed/
rX372ZwXOEM [105]" frameborder="0" allowfullscreen></iframe>
```

The only problem is that this transformation is not a part of the Joomla core package. If you want to use macros, you need to install additional extensions, mostly so called plug ins.

Content in a module?

When we created an article, we used the content component of Joomla. Another possibility to create content can be a module.

A module is a content element that can be positioned on your website. A menu, for example, needs a module to be displayed. The Login box is also a module. You can create as many modules with predefined functions as you need and position them in the predefined area in the template. Joomla comes with 24 pre-installed modules. You can see them with descriptions under *Extensions → Module Manager → New (Figure 7)*.

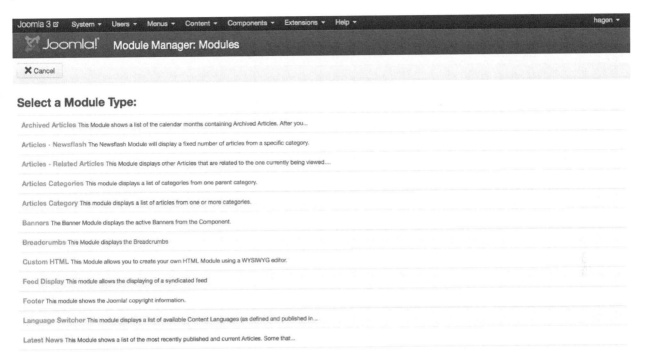

Figure 7: Available Modules

It is possible to create a module that contains HTML text like an article (*Custom HTML module*). And it is also possible to upload e.g. a background image for each module and to publish the module time based. It is not intended that custom HTML content in modules is created by "normal" authors. Content creation in modules is more a "Manager" or "Administrator" task. Try out the Custom HTML module. Create one, add some content and choose a position (*Figure 8*).

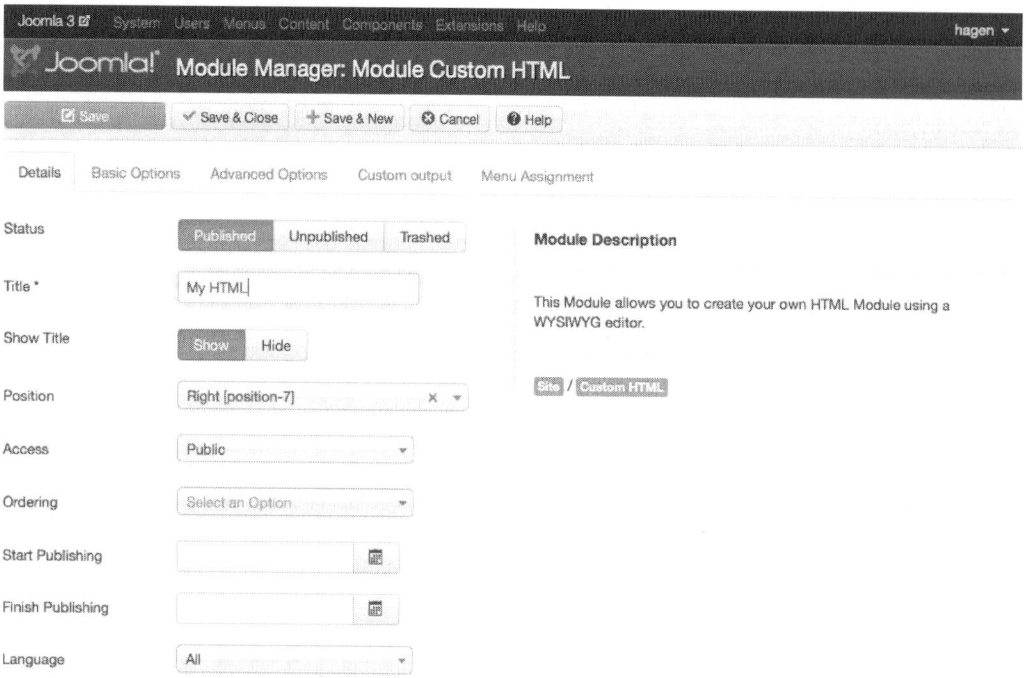

Figure 8: Custom HTML module in control panel

You can use the rich text editor and all the features that are available to write, format and enhance article text. You can even configure on which page the module should appear (tab *Menu Assignment*) and when it should appear (*time based publishing*).

After saving, your custom HTML module appears on your site (*Figure 9*).

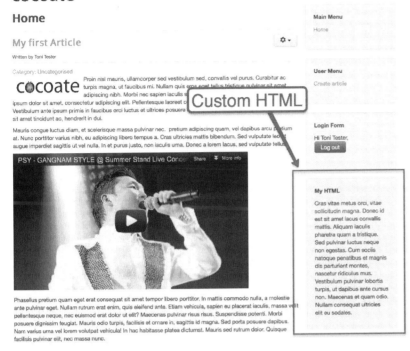

Figure 9: Custom HTML module on website

If more than one module is located at the same position it is necessary to bring them into the desired order. Just drag the modules in the module manager to the desired place (*Figure 10*).

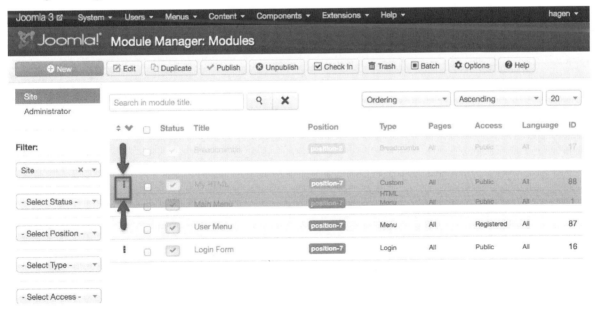

Figure 10: Sorting of modules

7. Display Content

After you managed to create content, you need to think about how displaying it. This sounds simple but it is quite important. In the last chapter we created an article and featured this article on the frontpage. Visitors can see the article only by visiting the front page.

THE FRONTPAGE

The standard frontpage (Home) has the menu item type Featured Articles. When you access the Main Menu in Menus → Menu Manager you probably noticed the little "home" symbol. It means, that this menu contains the link to the front page (*Figure 1*).

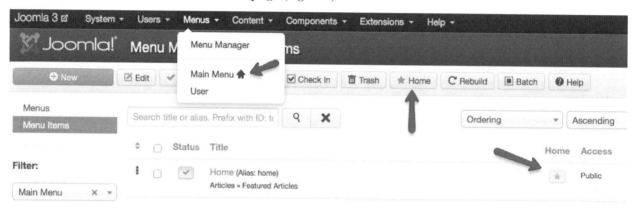

Figure 1: Main menu with Home link

You have different configuration options while editing the Home link. The featured articles menu item type offers leading articles, intro articles, columns and links. To understand how it works, we need a few articles. For the sake of simplicity in our example, just copy your first article. The copy process is possible in the Save dialog and in a batch dialog. Select the article you want to copy and click the Batch icon (*Figure 2*).

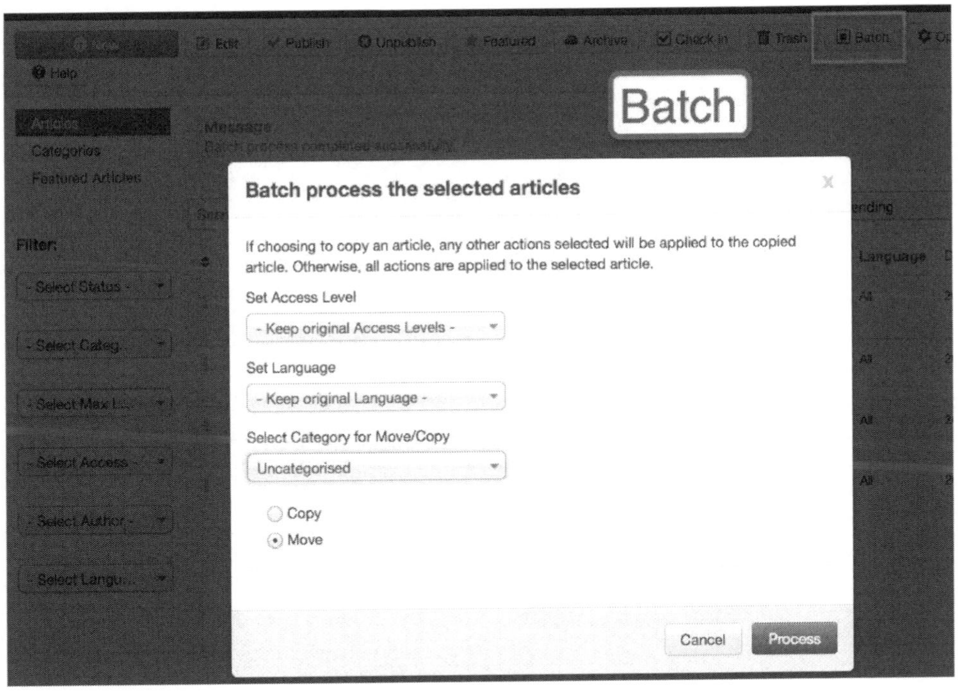

Figure 2: Copy articles in a batch

If you have more than 4-5 articles (don't forget to "feature" them), you can try out the different options. Go to *Menus → Main Menu → Home* and take a look at the *Advanced Options* tab. You can see 1 leading article, 3 intro articles in 3 columns (*Figure 3*).

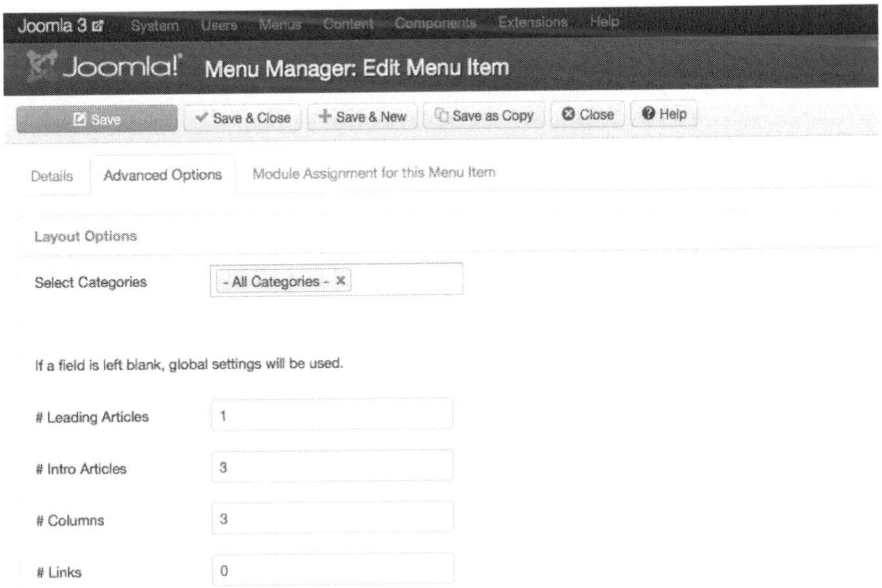

Figure 3: Layout in Home menu link

On your front page it appears like in *Figure 4*.

Figure 4: Default frontpage

CATEGORIES AND MENU LINKS

Joomla offers two possibilities to structure your content: Categories and Menu links. Each article belongs to one category. Categories can be nested. Menu links can point to articles or categories or they can point to a set of articles as with the featured articles for the frontpage. This simple and easy extendible structure offers amazing ways to display content.

As you already know, Joomla's templates are offering positions. Positions are places where you can place your content and your navigation elements.

Joomla's content display system is the arrangement of modules and the components on predefined templates positions.

Each page can have exactly one component and an unlimited amount of modules.

Categories can be created and managed in *Content → Categories*.

Menus can be created, managed and filled with links in *Menus → Menu Manager* (read more about creating a menu in chapter 5 - It's all about users, permissions, modules and articles

A NAVIGATION ON TOP

An empty Joomla page has a *"Main Menu"* at *position-7* in the default template. We use the Protostar template and there it is at *position-7* in the *right* sidebar, but we want to have the main menu on top. To achieve this goal, go to *Extensions* → *Module Manager* → *Main Menu* and move it to *position-1*. In the Advanced Options tab change the Menu Class Suffix to *" nav-pills"* (*there's a white space at the beginning!*) (*Figure 5*).

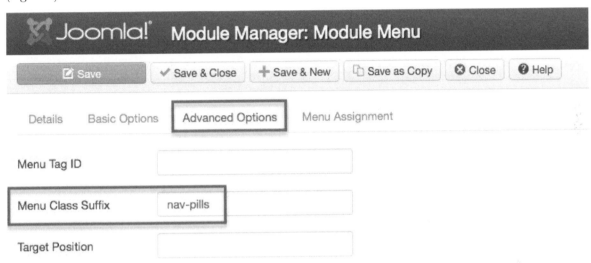

Figure 5: Menu Class Suffix

It will change the class attribute in the HTML code and when everything is correct, your navigation should look like in *Figure 6*.

Figure 6: Navigation with Main Menu

Articles in categories can be displayed in "blog style" like on the frontpage or as tables of articles. Both are highly configurable. You just need to check out a few menu item types.

With these few tools you can create amazing layouts.

8. Extensions

As we have already seen in the extension manager, the Joomla 3 package comes with many inbuilt extensions. We already came in touch with a few of them. As a website user, you probably don't care much about the extension you are using as long as it is working for you. However, as an administrator, you have to know exactly what is going on. We already looked at several Joomla! extensions like the content extension, which allows you to write and manage articles as well as publish them in different ways on the website. The user extension relates to users, the category extension to categories and so on.

In the Components menu, you will see Banners, Contacts, Joomla! Update, Messaging, Newsfeeds, Redirects, Search, Smart Search and Weblinks. We will have a short look at these components including related modules and plugins. As the handling is exactly the same as in Joomla 2.5, I just summarize the idea behind the component and link to a detailed description on our website based on Joomla 2.5.

BANNERS

The banner component provides the option to display advertising banners on your site. A banner can consist of graphics or custom HTML code. Every time your site is accessed, a different banner will be displayed from your banner collection. You can click on these banners and they are linked to the client's site. The banner component offers client, category, and banner administration as well as detailed analyses.

Read a detailed description of the banner component on our website[16] (Joomla 2.5)

CONTACTS

Every website needs a contact form. Sometimes you may need only one, sometimes more of these forms, depending on the provider of the website. A company website with more than one department may need to have a contact form for every department. Perhaps you need to have a contact form for every employee or every user account. All of this can be done by using the Joomla! contact component.

Read a description of the contact component on our website[17] (Joomla 2.5) and a how to build such a contact form[18].

JOOMLA UPDATE

---

[16] http://cocoate.com/node/10315

[17] http://cocoate.com/node/10316

[18] http://cocoate.com/node/10306

Here you can decide which branch of Joomla the **automatic update system** is following. You can choose between long term support, standard term support, testing or fully customized.

MESSAGING

Messaging is an inbuilt private messaging system for backend users and a core component of Joomla. It allows you to send and receive messages from other users which have the permission to access the administrator area. The messaging component is very easy to use; however, users often forget the possibility to configure the component in Components → Messages → My Settings. You can configure the system to email you every new message, delete them after an amount of days, and you can also lock your inbox.

NEWSFEEDS

Feeds are very handy. It is possible to subscribe to different kind of news and information. Unfortunately, even today, often people don't use them for some inexplicable reasons. Thirty years ago, you had to buy and read a newspaper to get to know the 'News'. Fifteen years ago you opened your browser and visited one website after another to get the "News". Today, you can still do both, but it's also possible to use a feed aggregator. Google's reader[19] and the dynamic bookmark toolbar of your browser (e.g. Firefox) are quite popular. The Joomla Newsfeeds component is an aggregator as well. Not so sophisticated as Google's reader, but also quite useful.

The news feed component allows you to collect feeds from other sites and publish them on your site.

In today's world of social media, everyone probably has dozens of user accounts. Often, videos and images are stored on youtube.com and flickr.com. In a company, the situation is even more complex. Imagine how much information is available in newsfeeds about a project like Joomla! or about your company.

Read a detailed description of the newsfeeds component on our website[20] (Joomla 2.5)

REDIRECTS

The redirect manager is a wonderful idea. It redirects a visitors to a valid page when they try to access a page that doesn't exist. It is possible that it existed before and was added to the search index of a search engine, or someone stored it at another website. This problem usually occurs after re-launching a website.

The redirect component is very convenient. If someone tries to access a path that doesn't exist, Joomla shows the 404 - not found page and simultaneously creates a new entry in the redirect manager. That makes the life for administrators easier to check non-working pages.

---

[19] http://www.google.com/reader

[20] http://cocoate.com/node/10318

Read a description of the redirects component on our website[21] (Joomla 2.5)

SEARCH

People expect to be able to search content on your website.

Joomla! uses by default a full text search. Full text means that Joomla! searches for all keywords you enter in the search box directly in the database.

This may sound obvious to most people, but it isn't. Many search engines create first a search index consisting of words used on your website. During the actual search, the search index is browsed for matches. These matches are linked to the actual content. The search result page is based on these matches and links.

Index-based search is faster than full text search but the index has to be updated with every website change, otherwise the new content cannot be found. In order to compensate for the performance advantage of the index-based search function, Joomla! is highly configurable.

Read a description of the search component on our website[22] (Joomla 2.5)

SMART SEARCH

Smart Search was a new feature in Joomla 2.5 and has been getting even better in Joomla 3.

It adds a "smarter" search engine to the Joomla core which is more flexible and faster with auto-completion and the "did you mean" feature (stemming).

> ### *Stemming?*
> *A stemmer for English, for example, should identify the string "cats" (and possibly "catlike",*
> *"catty" etc.) as based on the root "cat", and "stemmer", "stemming", "stemmed" as based on*
> *"stem". A stemming algorithm reduces the words "fishing", "fished", "fish", and "fisher" to the*
> *root word, "fish" (Wikipedia[23]).*

The Joomla core package comes with an English stemmer and the so called Snowball Stemmer (*Extensions→ Smart Search → Options*). The English stemmer works out of the box, the Snowball stemmer requires the Stem PHP extension and provides support for 14 languages including Danish, German, English, Spanish, Finnish, French, Hungarian, Italian, Norwegian, Dutch, Portuguese, Romanian, Russian, and Turkish.

The data need to be indexed in order to get this flexibility and speed.

Read a description of the smart search component on our website (Joomla 2.5)

---

[21] http://cocoate.com/node/10319

[22] http://cocoate.com/node/10320

[23] http://en.wikipedia.org/wiki/Stemming

WEBLINKS

With the weblinks component, you can create a link list or a download section for your website. To do so, Joomla! provides the nested categories system and counts the individual hits on the links. This component is useful for link catalogs. Add as many web link categories as you need, create as many web links as you have, then connect both by assigning categories. Add a menu link, choose a layout and configure the options. Read a description of the weblinks component on our website[24] (Joomla 2.5)

THIRD PARTY EXTENSIONS

In the Joomla extensions directory[25]you find more than 10,000 extensions to enhance your website with different features (*so far 613 are compatible with the new Joomla 3 series, Oct. 2012*). With the Extension Manager (*Extensions → Extension Manager*) you can install, update, discover and manage extensions directly from your Joomla administration.

MANAGING EXTENSIONS

You can install extensions in three different ways (*Figure 1*).

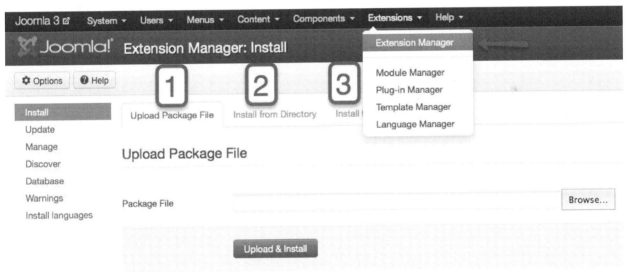

Figure 1: Installing extensions

- **Upload a Package file**
  If you have downloaded a zip file to your local PC that contains a Joomla extension, you can use this option to upload and install your extension.

---

[24] http://cocoate.com/node/10385

[25] http://extensions.joomla.org/

- **Install from Directory**

  If you have uploaded a zip file containing a Joomla! extension to the document root directory on your web server, you can use this option to extract and install your extension.

- **Install from URL**

  If you know the URL of a zip file that contains a Joomla extension, you can use this option to download, extract and install your extension

  There are screens for updating, managing (disable, uninstall) and for installing languages.

  The discover dialog allows you to check extensions that have not gone through the normal installation process. Using this feature you can upload extension files directly to your web server using some other means such as FTP or SFTP and place those extension files into the appropriate directory and install the extension.

9. Social Media and Cloud Computing

Both buzzwords are tied to each other. Social networks are not really possible without cloud computing and cloud computing is getting more social :)

SOCIAL MEDIA

Social media offers interactive dialogues and "introduce substantial and pervasive changes to communication between organizations, communities, and individuals."

Figure 1: Social Media

I'm sure you have a Facebook and a Google account. May be also one at Twitter, Flickr, Pinterest, Slideshare, LinkedIn, Vimeo and even more. Have a look at this presentation[26] to get an idea about these services.

Facebook offers Facebook pages for companies and individuals, Google offers Google+ pages for companies and individuals. Slideshows can be embedded via Slideshare, photos via Flickr, videos via YouTube and Vimeo) and even tweets from Twitter. These services offer badges which can be integrated in Joomla with iframes (Read more about embedding iframes in Joomla articles in chapter 6 - Create Content).

Most of these services are a mixture of social media and cloud based hosting of files. All the screenshots of these books are stored on Flickr[27].

There are two ways to access your data in these networks. One is the "iframe way" and the other is the "API way". An API is a programming interface and several third party Joomla extensions are using e.g. the Facebook API to implement a Facebook login. The Joomla core contains a plugin called Authentication - GMail (*Extensions → Plug In Manager*). It offers the user authentication with a GMail/ Googlemail account.

Generally, I think it is useful to write your content on your website and use social networks to talk about and link to your content.

---

[26] http://www.slideshare.net/hagengraf/social-media-13278371

[27] http://www.flickr.com/photos/hagengraf/sets/72157631559834633

CLOUD COMPUTING

Cloud computing is the use of computing resources (hardware and software) that are delivered as a service over the Internet. The name comes from the use of a cloud-shaped symbol as an abstraction of the complex infrastructure.

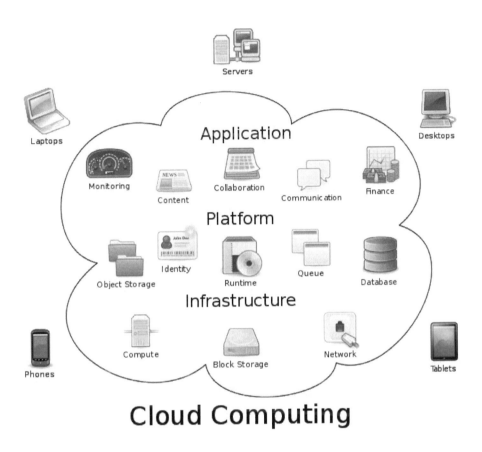

Figure 2 - Cloud Computing - en.wikipedia.org/wiki/Cloud_computing

You also can use cloud services to host your Joomla installation. More and more hosting companies start to offer a Joomla installation in the cloud.

In the main, I think cloud computing is useful to have an "easy to maintain" content base. You just have to ensure that it's possible to export your content in an easy way, in case you want to change your cloud computing provider.

10. Common tasks

This is a short book and the idea behind it was to tell you in 10 steps how to deal with Joomla 3. I hope, while reading it, you became more familiar with Joomla 3.

Nevertheless, I could add many more chapters for this book to explain all the details and nice little features Joomla is offering you.

You can build everything with Joomla! Have a look at the extension directory[28] and enhance your Joomla website with the feature you need.

However, I just want to mention a few very necessary extensions:

SEARCH ENGINE OPTIMIZATION

The following listed three options for search engine optimization are covered in Joomla core:

• Joomla core comes with SEO options (*System → Global Configuration → Site - SEO Settings*).

• You can set meta description for the whole site and for each article. A meta description is the brief summary of the content behind an URL that appears after performing an online search query. Even though it is not longer considered to be of key importance for search engine rankings, it influences the click-through rate of the link to your site in search results (i.e. whether or not users will actually feel feel like clicking on the link). Meta descriptions shouldn't be longer than 160 characters (*Article → Meta Data Options* tab).

• the redirect component (*Components → Redirect*)
Redirecting users from your old or non-existing pages, documents and other website assets to the new ones can be done in 3 easy steps using Joomla's native redirect component. It is user-friendly, has zero learning curve, and, most importantly, every time a visitor tries to access a non-existing page, the component stores its URL, or, if it has already been stored, starts counting attempts to access the page. You can then swiftly fix the problem by adding a new url to redirect future visitors to a page that works.

UPDATE

Joomla has an **automatic update system**. You just have to look in *Extensions → Extension Manager → Update*. Click the Find Updates button and install them with a mouse click

BACKUP AND RESTORE

---

[28] http://extensions.joomla.org/

You learn the importance of backing your data up if your computer or your web-server fails and you face rebuilding of your site from scratch. Depending on the severity of paranoia you suffer from, you might like to choose one of the following solutions:

• Your provider offers a backup and restore solution and you trust it

• Install a third party component like Akeeba backup[29]

• Use your own backup solution

RESSOURCES

You want to know more about Joomla?

Then this book was just a beginning for you ;-)

I hope, you enjoyed reading it. My intention was to guide you through the basics of Joomla! 3. If you want to acquire a more profound knowledge of the subject, read

• Joomla 2.5 - Beginner's Guide [30]

• Joomla! Development - Beginner's Guide[31]

• Going Mobile with Joomla[32]

All books are available in several languages as a **free PDF**.

Want to learn more about Joomla? Want to get in touch with Joomla! community? Here are some websites you might like to visit:

Community

Joomla! is backed by a worldwide community. If you like this idea, come and join us!

Become a member of http://community.joomla.org/

Read the community magazine at http://magazine.joomla.org/.

Maybe there is a Joomla! user group near you to join http://community.joomla.org/user-groups.html

If not, start one yourself!

Twitter: http://twitter.com/joomla

---

[29] http://www.akeebabackup.com/

[30] http://cocoate.com/node/10419

[31] http://cocoate.com/node/10106

[32] http://cocoate.com/node/10604

Facebook: http://www.facebook.com/joomla

Flickr: http://www.flickr.com/groups/joomla/

Documentation
http://docs.joomla.org/

Security Checklist
http://docs.joomla.org/Security_Checklist_1_-_Getting_Started

Joomla! Templates
There is no central directory for free templates.

There is no central directory for commercial templates.

Anyway, there are a lot of template clubs and professionals that provide Joomla! templates. Just search the web and you will for sure find something that suits you.

Events
Joomla! is known for its Joomla! days.

A Joomla! day is a one- or two-day event organized by and for the community. A list of Joomla! days can be found here - http://community.joomla.org/events.html

There is an international Joomla! conference in Europe called J and Beyond. Go to http://jandbeyond.org/ for more information.

From November 16-18, 2012, the first Joomla world conference[33] takes place in San Jose, USA

The Future
The community plans a six month release cycle, based on the ideas people post in the Joomla! idea pool[34]

The next long term release will be Joomla! 3.5 in 2013/2014

The Joomla! developer network is always looking for people like you :-)[35]

Training and Commercial Support
http://resources.joomla.org/directory/support-services/training.html

---

[33] http://conference.joomla.org/

[34] http://ideas.joomla.org/forums/84261-joomla-idea-pool

[35] http://developer.joomla.org/

http://resources.joomla.org/

http://cocoate.com

More books from cocoate

Joomla! 2.5 Beginner's Guide

Joomla! Development for Beginner's

Going Mobile with Joomla!

http://cocoate.com/publications

cocoate

www.cocoate.com

cocoate.com is the publisher of this book and an independent management consultancy, based in France and working internationally.

Specialized in three areas – Consulting, Coaching and Teaching – cocoate.com develops web based strategies for process and project management and public relations; provides customized trainings for open source content management systems Drupal, Joomla and WordPress, in the area of management and leadership skills and develops educational projects with the focus on non-formal learning.

The European educational projects focus on the promotion of lifelong learning with the goal of social integration. Particular emphasis is placed on learning methods in order to learn how to learn, the conception and realization of cross-generational learning strategies and local community development.

http://cocoate.com

Spend your holidays in Southern France

We were captive to the charme of this old French village from the beginning and that's why we live and work in Fitou. We restored an old village house into holiday apartments because we like to host guests and share with them our love for this region.

Fitou is situated in the South of France, between Perpignan and Narbonne and is a typical French wine village having guarded the distinctive architectural village houses. The region around Fitou is known for its wine and is as diverse as it can be, situated not too far from the Pyrenees (one hour drive) and Spain. The Mediterranean climate allows you to enjoy the freshness of the Mediterranean sea at one of the beautiful beaches enclosing the Étang from March until October, as Languedoc-Roussillon is the sunniest area in France. The country of Cathar offers not only old castles and abbeys but also the historical Canal du Midi.

Our apartments can be rented during the whole year. The apartments are part of an old traditional stone house in the heart of Fitou. They have been carefully restored and modernized, respecting architectural aspects and conforming to the neighboring houses. Feel free to discover our apartments and the region surrounding them!

http://fimidi.com

Made in the USA
San Bernardino, CA
13 November 2012